As We Gather,
As We Part

As We Gather, As We Part

150 New Opening and Closing Prayers

by
Carl Koch

Saint Mary's Press
Christian Brothers Publications
Winona, Minnesota

To Lou Anne, Virginia, Vicki, and Janet,
who have supported and guided me
through beginnings and endings.

Genuine recycled paper with 10% post-consumer waste.
Printed with soy-based ink.

The publishing team included Laurie A. Berg, copy editor; James H. Gurley, production editor and typesetter; Maurine R. Twait, art director; Sue Campbell, cover designer; pre-press, printing, and binding by the graphics division of Saint Mary's Press.

The acknowledgments continue on page 72.

Printed in the United States of America

Printing: 9 8 7 6 5 4 3 2 1

Year: 2006 05 04 03 02 01 00 99 98

ISBN 0-88489-496-7

Contents

Introduction

As We Gather, As We Part will prove useful to anyone who is asked to start or end a meeting, a class, or a small community gathering with a prayer, but does not have time to prepare one. The prayers in this book touch on the key themes of Christian life, and each prayer can easily be adapted to various situations.

One important feature of the prayers is that they each include a passage from the Bible. By including biblical passages, the prayers not only set our attention on God but also proclaim God's word. The prayers give us words with which to communicate with God and provide us with a way to listen to what God is telling us.

Using These Prayers

At the beginning of each section of prayers, three opening statements are offered to call the gathering into God's presence. Select the opening Call to presence that best fits the prayer you have chosen and the circumstances in which you are praying. Pausing briefly after the Call to presence allows for recollection and calming before the prayer proper. Most people appreciate this peaceful pause.

Read the selected prayer slowly but naturally. Permit the words to sink in. If a pause is indicated—particularly in the "Ask and Receive" chapter—take it.

Practicing the prayers beforehand will enhance their effectiveness. Being familiar with the prayer becomes even more important if it is to be read over a public address system.

After you have read a prayer, you may wish to add a short prayer of your own to personalize it for the community. For instance, after a prayer of praise and thanksgiving, you might say something like, "Tonight, we thank God especially for . . ."

In many of the prayers, the last line serves as a good ending, but a distinct closing line is also provided for each chapter of prayers. So, to end a prayer, just use the final line of the prayer, use the ending line given at the end of each chapter, or create an ending of your own.

Finally, these prayers may serve you well as

- morning or evening prayers
- meal prayers
- parts of longer prayer services
- sources of reflection or meditation
- prayers for any occasion

It is hoped that however you use these prayers, they will help you and your community communicate with God and listen to God's word.

CHAPTER 1

Ask and Receive

Call to presence

- We recall your presence with us, merciful God.
- Let us remember that the God of abundant blessings is with us and hears our prayer.
- Come, God of faithful love, be with us as we gather.

Prayers

Note: The bracketed statements offer a place to add particular petitions that you may want to offer for a group.

Matthew 7:7–8 _____

All through the story of our salvation, we have called on you, God, and you have answered. Jesus tells us: "Ask, and it will be given you; search, and you will find; knock, and the door will be opened for you. For everyone who asks receives."

As we gather now, we need your help, gracious God. We ask you in particular for guidance and peace. [Offer any petitions for the group now.] And, in the silence of our heart, we each ask for what we need right now. [Pause briefly.] Hear us once again, our God.

Mark 11:22–24 _____

God, you have always been faithful to us. When we ask you anything in faith, you show your overwhelming love for us. As Jesus tells us:

> Have faith in God. Truly I tell you, if you say to this mountain, "Be taken up and thrown into the sea," and if you do not doubt in your heart, but believe that what you say will come to pass, it will be done for you. So I tell you, whatever you ask for in prayer, believe that you have received it, and it will be yours.

First, Holy One, we ask for the faith to move mountains. May our heart be filled with such conviction. [We also offer you these petitions.] In silence and with faith, we each ask for the graces we need. [Pause briefly.] Thank you, living God, for hearing our prayers.

Luke 11:11–13 _____

Over and over, God, you have delivered your people from their troubles. Your mercy is too generous to understand. Jesus declared: "Is there anyone among you who, if your child asks for a fish, will give a snake instead of a fish? . . . If you then, . . . know how to give good gifts to your children, how much more will [God] give the Holy Spirit to those who ask."

We seek your Holy Spirit now. Come, Spirit of God, be with us. Teach us the truth of the Gospels; send us the wisdom of God. [In particular, we offer these prayers of petition.] Holy Spirit, each of us has need of your help, and so, individually and silently, we ask for the aid that we need. [Pause briefly.] Thanks and praise to you, God of endless mercy.

John 14:12–14 _____

Jesus tells his disciples and those of us gathered here: "I tell you, the one who believes in me will also do the works that I do and, in fact, will do greater works than these. . . . I will do whatever you ask in my name. . . . If in my name you ask me for anything, I will do it."

Saving God, we find it hard to imagine that we could do works greater than Jesus could do. Nevertheless, we have his word for it, and his word is truth. In Jesus' name we pray for your continued grace so that we might have faith, love, and hope. [As we gather, we pray particularly for these needs . . .] In the silence of our heart, grant each of us the grace that we need right now. [Pause briefly.] All these things we pray for in the name of Christ Jesus.

John 15:5–7

God of mercy, abide in us so that we may have the confidence to pray as Jesus tells us to pray. In John's Gospel, he says: "Those who abide in me and I in them bear much fruit, because apart from me you can do nothing. . . . If you abide in me, and my words abide in you, ask for whatever you wish, and it will be done for you."

And so we ask most importantly that you dwell in our heart. May all of us bear the fruits of your grace. [As we come together, we especially make these requests of you . . .] We pray, silently and hopefully, for our own specific needs. [Pause briefly.] Come, God of life, abide with us.

James 1:5–6

You, God, always welcome our cries for help. Moses, Ruth, Elijah, Esther, Jeremiah, and Judith needed your help and got it. As the Scriptures say: "If any of you is lacking in wisdom, ask God, who gives to all generously and ungrudgingly, and it will be given you. But ask in faith, never doubting."

As people in need, we gather in your presence. We have faith, but we ask for more of it. We have some understanding, but we ask for deeper wisdom. [Now, we also ask for these particular needs . . .] As individuals and in the privacy of our heart, we ask you, God, for what we need. [Pause briefly.] All praise and thanks to you, Source of all goodness.

1 John 3:21–22

Your generosity to us, Holy One, is larger than we can comprehend. You invite us to pray boldly. As the Scriptures say, "If our hearts do not condemn us, we have boldness before God; and we receive . . . whatever we ask."

Those who have gathered with you now are not blameless, and we hope that our heart is ready for your grace. So, in the quiet of our heart, we place these needs before you. [Pause briefly.] Send us a deeper faith. [We place the needs of all gathered here in your hands.] Blessings and thanks be to you, God of all creation.

Psalm 21:2–4 _____

With confidence in your care for us, we pray this psalm to you, God of the universe:

> You [God] have granted me my heart's desire;
> you refused not the wish of my lips.
>
> . . . .
> I asked life of you:
> you gave me length of days forever and ever.

You always answer our prayer with goodness in mind for us. Sometimes we do not comprehend your replies, but we trust in your will. We gather with you, our God, and each of us makes petition to you for the needs we have. [Pause briefly.] We ask fullness of life from you, our God. [And we set before you these petitions for the good of us all.] We bless you, Source of all goodness.

Psalm 20:4–9 _____

God, your people prayed this psalm, asking guidance for their leaders. We pray it now, asking you to lead us.

> May God grant you what your heart desires
> and fulfill all your plans.
> May we shout for joy over your triumph
> and in the name of our God wave our banners;
> may Yahweh fulfill all your petitions.
>
> . . . .
> Save us, Yahweh;
> answer when we call.

We stumble into error and trouble unless you guide us. Save us, living God. We each have needs that we pray for now in the quiet of our heart. [Pause briefly.] Fulfill all our petitions. [We ask particularly for your help with these petitions . . .] We declare our thanks to you, our God.

Proverbs 8:17–18 _____

Holy God, in Proverbs you tell us:

> I love those who love me,
>   and those who seek me diligently find me.
> Riches and honor are with me,
>   enduring wealth and prosperity.

We come together to seek your will, and we desire the fruits of doing good. May we always find your love. [Right now, our God, we seek your presence and your help with these needs . . .] In the privacy of our heart, we each ask you for the graces that we need. [Pause briefly.] All honor and praise to you, Source of every good thing.

Jeremiah 29:12–13 _____

Loving God, you never want us to drift away from you. Even when the people of Israel turned their back on you, you told them: "When you call upon me and come and pray to me, I will hear you. When you search for me, you will find me; if you seek me with all your heart."

We seek you, we call upon you, our God. Even though, like the people of Israel, we sometimes turn our back on you, we trust that you never turn your back on us. So, once again, we ask for your grace and guidance. [In particular we ask for your help with these concerns . . .] Silently we each offer our petitions to you, gracious God. [Pause briefly.]

Matthew 6:11–12 _____

We offer you, our Creator, these words from the prayer that Jesus taught us:

> Give us this day our daily bread.
> And forgive us our debts,
>   as we also have forgiven our debtors.

We always come to you with our needs. You always listen and answer. [Today we come to you with these needs . . .] In the silence of our heart, we ask you to give us what we need. [Pause briefly.] We pledge in turn to be people of service and forgiveness.

2 Corinthians 6:1–2 _____

Source of all wisdom, we gather in your name again. May we keep in mind your constant care for us and Paul's words: "As we work together with [Jesus], we urge you also not to accept the grace of God in vain. For [God] says, 'At an acceptable time I have listened to you, and on a day of salvation I have helped you.'"

We wish to work together with Jesus, because without him we can do nothing good. [Specifically we ask for these things . . .] Individually we offer you these petitions. [Pause briefly.] Glory and praise to you, our God.

Isaiah 41:9–10 _____

We have no God but you, Creator of the universe. Be with us just as you promised in Isaiah:

> "You are my servant,
> I have chosen you and not cast you off";
> do not fear, for I am with you,
> do not be afraid, for I am your God;
> I will strengthen you, I will help you.

With steadfast hope we call on you, our God, for help. Help us to put aside any fear in the sure knowledge that you love us and dwell with us. [In addition, we ask for these needs

. . .] We also offer these individual petitions, praying in the silence of our heart. [Pause briefly.] Blessed are you, God of the universe.

Psalm 40:4–5,16–17 _____

In the words of the psalmist, we offer you this prayer, our God:

> Happy those who put their trust in Yahweh.
>
> . . . .
>
> How many wonders you have done for us.
>
> . . . .
>
> To all who love your saving power
> give constant cause to say, "God be glorified."
> To me, afflicted and poor,
> come quickly.
> My Helper, my Savior, my God,
> come and do not delay!

We do put our trust in you, our God. Come, do not delay to help us in our need. Save us from straying from your path. [In particular, we ask your help in these matters . . .] In the privacy of our heart, we seek your help. [Pause briefly.] You are our helper, our savior, and our only God. All praise and thanks to you.

Ending

In complete trust that you will hear and answer us with love, we lift our voices to you, ever faithful God. Amen.

CHAPTER 2

Be Reconciled

Call to presence

- Let us remember that the Prince of Peace dwells among us at this moment.

- God, source of forgiveness and reconciliation, be with us now as we pray.

- Forgiving God, be with us now.

Prayers

2 Corinthians 5:18–20 _____

Merciful God, you call us to be reconcilers. Paul told the divid-ed people of Corinth: "God . . . has given us the ministry of reconciliation; . . . entrusting the message of reconciliation to us. So we are ambassadors for Christ."

As we gather may we take these words to heart and put them into practice. Let us be ambassadors, representatives of Christ in the way we treat one another. May we be forces of unity and peace, truth and charity with one another. Only through your grace is this possible, so guide and direct us with your power.

Genesis 50:19–20 _____

In the Book of Genesis, Joseph forgave his brothers even though they had sold him into slavery. He reassured them: "Do not be afraid! Even though you intended to do harm to me, God intended it for good."

God, you can always bring good from evil. One of the greatest evils is having a hard heart toward those who have done us wrong. By forgiving, we, too, can see what good can come from a bad situation. Lead us to have a forgiving spirit and a wider perspective so that we can see and do good. Then, like Joseph, we can say, "Do not be afraid," and no one will need to be.

Nehemiah 9:17 _____   _____

Forgiving God, even when the people of Israel continually wandered from the ways of righteousness, you forgave them. As Nehemiah says, "You are a God ready to forgive, gracious and merciful, slow to anger and abounding in steadfast love, and you did not forsake [sinful Israel]."

As we gather together, God of mercy, help us to forgive one another readily and gladly. May we be as courteous, gracious, and trustworthy as you have been forever. God, never abandon us to our anger and grudges and the destruction they cause. Rather, plant in our heart your forgiving, generous spirit.

Adapted from Psalm 65:2–3 _____

All of us sin. Virtue eludes us. As the psalmist says: "All flesh comes to God burdened with sin, overwhelmed with failings. Even so, God pardons human shortcomings."

God, we do wrong in a million ways, some small and some large. We tell small fibs and big lies. We spread rumors and even slander. We ignore the hungry and pollute the earth. Help us to admit our sins and to open our heart to your grace, the grace we need to turn back to your way, your truth, your life. And, realizing our own need for forgiveness, may we be forgiving of the faults of other people.

Luke 6:37 _____

Jesus warned his followers: "Do not judge, and you will not be judged; do not condemn, and you will not be condemned. Forgive, and you will be forgiven."

Merciful God, we find it easy to pass judgment on other people without trying to understand them. We hate to be judged ourselves, but we often judge others. Then we pass sentence. God, open our heart and mind to other people. Help us to listen, to put aside our biases, so that we can come to a better understanding of our neighbors. And may we readily forgive, just as you forgive us. It's not easy, but with your grace it is possible.

Luke 11:4 _____

The Lord's Prayer asks God to "forgive us our sins, / as we ourselves forgive [those who trespass against] us."

Living God, how often are we really honest when we pray those lines? Surely we want your forgiveness, but do we really forgive those who have trashed our reputation, betrayed our trust, or done us other harm? Maybe we do sometimes, but more often we probably don't forgive others. Something in us wants revenge, or what we may think of as "our rights." God, shower us with your grace so that when we say "as we forgive those who trespass against us," we are speaking our reality and not just pious words.

Adapted from Luke 17:3–4 _____

God of mercy, Jesus gave us some hard commands. Here is one that we find especially difficult: "If people sin, counsel the sinners to reform. If the sinners change, forgive them. Even if they sin against you seven times every day, but repent each time, you must forgive them."

God, that is asking a lot of us. So much in our culture tells us just the opposite: "Don't get mad, get even" or "Fool me once, shame on you; fool me twice, shame on me." We're not supposed to forgive, we're supposed to get even. Instead, faithful God, teach us how to lead ourself and our neighbors to reform our ways and to forgive one another. We cannot learn such forgiveness without you, our God.

Luke 23:34 _____

From his cross Jesus cried out, "Father, forgive them; for they do not know what they are doing." He asked your forgiveness, God, for all the people who wanted to see him suffer, be crucified among criminals, and die a long and torturous death.

We excuse ourselves when we need forgiveness by claiming that we didn't know what we were doing. But all too often, we won't give anyone else the benefit of the doubt. And so we refuse forgiveness. God, give us the heart and will of your Son, Jesus. Help us to be forgiving. We know that we are responsible for our actions, but in the heat of the moment, we often act out of ignorance, anger, fear, and desperation. Give us a heart and mind ready to forgive as Jesus did.

Colossians 3:13 _____

To the Colossians Paul said: "Bear with one another and, if anyone has a complaint against another, forgive each other; just as [God] has forgiven you, so you also must forgive."

In all honesty, all-good God, we would probably offend one another less if we had more tolerance. Grant us the grace to be tolerant. Then, if we still argue, help us to forgive. We are not you, God, but you give us the grace to imitate your forgiveness. Be with us, forgiving God, as we forgive others.

Sirach 28:2 _____

Merciful God, you promise pardon of our sins when we forgive others. Sirach says:

> Forgive your neighbor the wrong he [or she] has done,
>   and then your sins will be pardoned when you
>   pray.
> Does anyone harbor anger against another, and expect
>   healing from [God]?

Huck Finn declares that we cannot pray a lie. Well, gracious God, that applies here, too. We can hardly pray for your forgiveness if we have no forgiveness for our neighbors. Healing comes when we forgive. So, God, teach us to forgive, and give us the courage and compassion to do so.

Ephesians 4:26,32 _____

Paul told the community at Ephesus: "Be angry but do not sin; do not let the sun go down on your anger. . . . Be kind to one another . . . and forgiving."

God, you inspired Paul to give this wise advice. If we do not seek to forgive and be done with our anger, it causes us no end of sleeplessness. We brood, and our anger grows. Instead, help us to deal with conflict right away, to do what we can to settle matters peacefully, to forgive one another, and to get on with living. Come, Spirit of God, give us hearts of kindness, forgiveness, and peace.

Colossians 1:20 _____

Saving God, you sent Jesus to bring us back into harmony with you and with one another. As the Scriptures say, "Through him God was pleased to reconcile . . . all things, whether on earth or in heaven, by making peace."

You send us into the world to follow in the footsteps of Jesus. Our attempts to make peace, bring people together, and act in harmony for the good of all our brothers and sisters is pleasing in your sight. Help us to take up the banner of peace and to extend our hands and help to one another.

2 Corinthians 13:13 _____

God, your servant Paul often ended his letters to the churches by saying, "The grace of the Lord Jesus Christ, the love of God, and the communion of the Holy Spirit be with all of you."

May this serve as our greeting and our farewell to one another. May we always seek grace, love, and communion with all people. In particular, as we gather together now, may we keep Paul's words in mind: *grace, love, communion.* Let them be our goal and our way with one another.

Colossians 2:2 _____ _____

God of all unity, our mission as Christians is well summarized in Paul's words to the Colossians, "I want their hearts to be encouraged and united in love, so that they may have all the riches of assured understanding and have the knowledge of . . . Christ."

We will never understand Christ without love for one another. So grant us the grace to be united in charity, respect, service, and worship. Whenever we gather, may people say of us, "See how these Christians love one another."

Ephesians 4:1–3 _____ _____

"Lead a life worthy of the calling to which you have been called," Paul reminds us, "with all humility and gentleness, with patience, bearing with one another in love, making every effort to maintain the unity of the Spirit in the bond of peace."

This is the calling to which we are called: unity of the Spirit. It is no easy task, and it is certainly not one that we can do on our own. So, once again, gracious God, we turn to you. Send your abundant blessings upon us as we gather so that we are, indeed, worthy of the calling to which you have called all of us.

Ending

We offer this prayer in the name of Jesus, prince of peace and source of all reconciliation. Amen.

CHAPTER 3

Listen, and Speak Truth

Call to presence

- Come, God, be with us in the full power of your truth.

- Let us remember that God, who always listens, is with us.

- Spirit of truth, may we recall that you are here with us now.

Prayers

Exodus 23:20–21 _____

God, you told the people of Israel in Exodus: "I am going to send an angel in front of you, to guard you on the way and to bring you to the place that I have prepared. Be attentive to him and listen to his voice."

    We may not be angels, Holy One, but you do call us to bring one another to the place you have prepared for us—your Reign of justice, love, and peace. May we be attentive to one another and to your Spirit present in each of us. May we listen to one another with the same respect that the people of Israel gave to your messenger.

Psalm 34:11–13 _____

God, you want us to listen carefully to one another but also to speak the truth. As the psalmist says:

Come, sons and daughters, listen to me,
I will teach you reverence for Yahweh.

. . . .

Keep your tongue from evil and your lips from speaking
    deceit.

We can hear the voice of God in the wisdom of one another, but we must listen. In turn, God directs us to speak honestly and to refrain from words that hurt and manipulate. May we listen and speak as God wills for us. This is the way of true wisdom.

Ephesians 4:25–26

As we come together, we seek the graces that we need in order to do as Paul urges: "Putting away falsehood, let all of us speak the truth to our neighbors, for we are members of one another. Be angry but do not sin; do not let the sun go down on your anger."

Source of all truth, help us to speak the truth, remembering that we are part of the Body of Christ. And, if we do grow angry with one another, help us to forgive instead of turning to sarcasm, sniping, hateful words, or worse. May we always keep before us as a prayer, "We are members of one another."

Proverbs 31:8–9

God, you urge us to:

    Speak out for those who cannot speak,
        for the rights of all the destitute.
    Speak out, judge righteously,
        defend the rights of the poor and needy.

May your words be a challenge to us as we come together. Let us recall the rights of those who are not with us, especially people who are poor or powerless. No matter what agenda we have, may our concern always be for the good of all your people.

Luke 10:16 _____

Holy One, we claim that we are disciples of Christ Jesus. We gather in the name of Jesus today. This claim of discipleship brings with it the responsibility to listen carefully to one another, as if we were listening to you. Jesus said, "Whoever listens to you [disciples] listens to me, and whoever rejects you rejects me, and whoever rejects me rejects the one who sent me."

In our time together, may we listen to one another with all the respect and attention that we would give to Jesus. In this way we will be true disciples and hear the words of everlasting life.

Sirach 6:33 _____

Your words are truth and life, Holy Wisdom. So the Book of Sirach tells us, "If you love to listen you will gain knowledge, / and if you pay attention you will become wise."

Help us learn to listen attentively, Source of all wisdom. Listening does not always come easy. Help us to remember these words from the Scriptures so that when we listen we will learn, and when we pay attention we will be planting the seeds of wisdom. God, help us to listen and attend.

Isaiah 1:10 _____

Saving God, you sent the prophets to the people of Israel to save them from their own mistakes and rebellions. The prophets started by telling people to listen. Isaiah declared:

> Hear the word of [God],
>   you rulers of Sodom.
> Listen to the teaching of our God,
>   you people of Gomorrah!

The people of neither city listened, and we know what happened to them. May we be less foolish and listen to your words, not only to those spoken in the Scriptures but also to the words of truth and charity spoken by our sisters and brothers. Give us ears to hear the prophet in one another.

Matthew 13:13 _____

Jesus explained to his disciples, "The reason I speak to them in parables is that 'seeing they do not perceive, and hearing they do not listen, nor do they understand.'"

As we gather, loving God, may we choose words that we can all understand. May we communicate clearly so that we will all be wiser and better. Jesus taught us to tell stories, so strengthen us to share our stories and our experiences.

Proverbs 10:20–21 _____

God, your word in the Scriptures says:

> The tongue of the righteous is choice silver;
> the mind of the wicked is of little worth.
> The lips of the righteous feed many,
> but fools die for lack of sense.

When we talk with one another, may we offer only words of choice silver. God of truth, grant that our words may nourish the soul of one another. Thus, we will all grow in wisdom and understanding. All of us are of infinite value; may our words honor you, God, by their kindness, honesty, and care.

Matthew 15:11 _____

Holy One, you sent Jesus to warn us that "it is not what goes into the mouth that defiles a person, but it is what comes out of the mouth that defiles."

Create clean hearts and generous minds in us so that whatever comes from our mouth may be considerate, just, and honest. In this way we can avoid being examples of "garbage in, garbage out." May we do our inner work so that our words will be filled with the Spirit of wisdom.

Ecclesiastes 10:12–13 _____

God, you hear every desire of our heart. We ask you, God, to give us the grace to keep in mind these words from the Scriptures:

Words spoken by the wise bring them favor,
  but the lips of fools consume them.
The words of their mouths begin in foolishness,
  and their talk ends in wicked madness.

Help us guard against our impulse to speak in haste, in anger, or in ignorance. Instead, may our words be offered in humility, in charity, and with understanding. Rather than being consumed by the sound of our own voice, may we be nourished by the words we share with one another.

Hebrews 3:12–13 _____

Living God, let us always hear your voice spoken, as it is in the Scriptures, by one another in all your creation. More than simply hearing, may we listen to your voice attentively with our heart. As Paul says: "Take care, brothers and sisters, that none of you may have an evil, unbelieving heart that turns away from the living God. But exhort one another every day."

Cleanse our heart of all that might make us cold, withdrawn, bitter, snide, sarcastic, or crude. Instead, guide our words so that they provide encouragement and hope for one another.

Sirach 5:11–14 _____

When we listen and speak, eternal God, may we be steady and strong in goodness. As the Scriptures say:

Be quick to hear,
  but deliberate in answering.
If you know what to say, answer your neighbor,

. . . .

Do not be called double-tongued
  and do not lay traps with your tongue.

First, help us to listen carefully. Then, Holy One, when we speak may we be clear and honest. Also, help us to have the humility to hold our tongue when we have nothing to contribute. Come, aid us with the gifts of listening and speaking.

Luke 22:51

God of all healing, Jesus performed many miraculous cures and told us to heal the sick and suffering. He wanted us to be cured not only of our physical deafness but also of our spiritual deafness. Even when Peter cut off the ear of the soldier who had come to arrest him, Jesus "touched his ear and healed him."

For those of us who are spiritually deaf, healing God, open our ears. Grant that we may hear your invitations to grace when they come through the Scriptures, nature, friendships, and every gathering of faith, such as this one. Touch our ears and heal us.

James 3:5,10

Creator God, you blessed us with the gift of speech, but as it is with any gift, we can misuse it. The Apostle James says, "The tongue is a small member, yet it boasts of great exploits. . . . From the same mouth come blessing and cursing."

Help us, our Creator, to use our voice for blessing, encouraging, reasoning, praising, and thanking. May we always lift up our voice in joyful song to thank you for all your abundant gifts to us. May the great exploits of our tongue be words of truth and love.

Ending

We lift our voices to our God, who gathers us together in the name of Jesus. Amen.

CHAPTER 4

Love Is the Key

Call to presence

- God, who is love, is now with us as we gather.
- Come, Fire of love and Light to our life. Be with us now.
- Let us remember that the God of love is present with us.

Prayers

Adapted from Proverbs 11:24–25 _____

God of all goodness, teach us generosity. In Proverbs you declare: "People give generously and still prosper. Others guard what is due to their neighbors and only end up wanting. Generous people will be enriched. Those who share water will receive water."

In all our dealings with one another, may we prosper by sharing generously. Grant us, generous God, open hearts and hands. May we trust your words. So, instead of protecting what we have, may we be willing to share with a glad heart.

Adapted from Acts of the Apostles 20:35 _____

As we gather together, may we keep Paul's words clearly in our heart: "We have to aid those too weak to help themselves, always recalling the words of Jesus that 'Giving is more blessed than receiving.'"

God of life, we have heard these words before. Now help us to act on them. In a quiet, competent, peaceful way, may we have the generosity to share what we can with a cheerful spirit and a willing heart. Help us to celebrate our power for good by giving to people who need our help. Bless you, God of all goodness, for our ability to share with our neighbor.

Hosea 11:4 _____

Forgiving God, all through history you have forgiven our evil ways and led us back to you. To your lost people, you declared, "I led them with cords of human kindness [and] bands of love."

Give us kind and forgiving hearts so that we may bring our sisters and brothers back from depression, loneliness, despair, and hatred. May we be your "bands of love." God of all goodness, may we never forget that you constantly forgive us and invite us to love.

Ezekiel 36:26 _____

Loving God, you created us to love one another and to love you. Indeed, you declared, "A new heart I will give you, and a new spirit I will put within you." Give us new hearts, warm hearts, lively spirits, ready spirits, so that we can love one another as you have loved us.

Help us to put aside anything that will turn our heart to stone: old resentments, grudges, worn-out fears, or distrust. In gathering together we need a new heart. Create this willing spirit within each of us.

John 15:12–15 _____

God, you brought us into a new and intimate relationship with you through Jesus, who tells us: "This is my commandment, that you love one another as I have loved you. . . . I do not call you servants any longer, . . . I have called you friends."

Well, God, all of us are commonplace, frail, ordinary humans. Help us to treat one another as we would treat Jesus. Let us welcome one another and serve one another with all the kindness, respect, and generosity that we would offer to Christ. Let us be true friends of one another.

Matthew 9:36 _____

God of compassionate love, may we follow Jesus' example. The Gospel tells us that when Jesus "saw the crowds, he had compassion for them, because they were harassed and helpless, like sheep without a shepherd." His compassion took the form of sharing the Good News, healing the people, and freeing them from bondage.

Send your spirit of compassion to us so that we may deal charitably with one another and with all our sisters and brothers. Because we often feel harassed and helpless, too, we need your shepherding to be good shepherds ourselves.

Mark 8:2 _____

God of abundant blessings, all of us need food for the body and for the spirit. In your love for humanity, you sent Jesus to be your love and to teach us how to love. He fed us, body and soul. After he had shared the Good News with a large crowd, he said, "I have compassion for the crowd, because they have been with me now for three days and have nothing to eat." Jesus had the disciples share what they had, and soon everyone was filled with food.

May we care enough for one another to feed one another's spirit with words of kindness and truth and to feed one another's body by sharing what food we have.

Luke 7:12–13

God-always-with-us, you call us to charity and compassion even in the face of death. When a widow had her dead son carried before Jesus, he did not ignore her sorrow. Instead, "he had compassion for her and said, 'Do not weep.'" Then he brought her son back to life.

Give us a compassionate spirit that moves us not only to kind words but to kind deeds as well. We may not have Jesus' power to raise the dead, but we can extend the hand of compassion. With your grace we can grieve with the sorrowful and help to raise crushed spirits. Send your grace of compassion.

1 Corinthians 12:13

Listen. "For in the one Spirit we were all baptized into one body . . . and we were all made to drink of one Spirit." Paul's words are a challenge to us to put aside any prejudices that we have, to lay down our defenses with one another, and to start working together for the common good.

One God, you call for us to be united in the one Spirit of Christ. May we respond to your call with an open mind, a willing heart, and ready hands. But first, help us to accept this fact: that we share the one Spirit of the baptized. We are all part of the Body of Christ.

Acts 9:36

God of love, you created us to love. All the Apostles and holy women and men throughout history have known this. When Jesus or the disciples wanted to praise someone, they pointed to the person's charity. As it says in Acts: "In Joppa there was a disciple whose name was Tabitha. . . . She was devoted to good works and acts of charity."

God, give us the grace to do good works and acts of love, so that when we come to the end of our life, we can look back and realize that we have not wasted it. Love gives substance to our faith in you. Help us, God who is love.

1 Timothy 1:3–5 _____

Creator of the universe, all of Jesus' teachings urge us to love even our enemies. Paul tells Timothy: "I urge you . . . to remain in Ephesus so that you may instruct certain people. . . . The aim of such instruction is love that comes from a pure heart, a good conscience, and sincere faith."

May our charity for one another be sincere, motivated by grace, and filled with faith. Moreover, God, send us grace that our love will be universal, inclusive of all our sisters and brothers, no matter what their race, religion, ethnic background, looks, or residence. Let us put nothing in the way of charity.

Luke 6:35 _____

God, your call to love is not always simple or easy, especially when Jesus says, "Love your enemies, do good, and lend, expecting nothing in return." It's one thing to love a friend, to show compassion for a sick person, or to be kind to a child. It's quite another to show compassion to someone we despise or to someone who has hurt us.

You promised us all the grace we would need. So, God of all power, send us your power to follow Jesus' command to love our enemies, to do good, and to give. This is tough love, but we can do it with your grace.

1 John 4:20 _____

God of truth, we cannot love you and not love other people. As the Scriptures say, "Those who say, 'I love God,' and hate their brothers or sisters, are liars; for those who do not love a brother or sister whom they have seen, cannot love God whom they have not seen." Once again you challenge us to be consistent.

God, help us to remember your words when we find ourselves tempted to haggle, spout angry slurs, manipulate, or just turn someone off. In our heart we want to love you and other people, so send your help that we might do so.

Sirach 6:16 _____

Holy Friend, you tell us in the Scriptures that "Faithful friends are life-saving medicine; / and those who fear [God] will find them." Truly, friends are lifesaving and life-giving. Thank you, God, for the gift of friendship.

Teach us how to be better friends to one another. Let us be people who share our values, support one another, listen, and help one another in substantial ways. You, God, sent Jesus to show us your friendship. Grace us with the same wisdom, will, and heart so that we may be a friend like Jesus.

Mark 10:21 _____

God, you sent Jesus to draw your people into the service of their poor, sick, and suffering sisters and brothers. Not only did Jesus identify with the poor, but he told the rich young man, "Go, sell what you own, and give the money to the poor, and you will have treasure in heaven; then come, follow me."

All of us who call ourselves Christians have before us the challenge of these words. Jesus, our savior, is in poor people, and he calls us to move from good intentions to deeds of loving service. We cannot do this alone. Only your grace makes such love possible. Fill us with this grace, God, that we may be effective in our compassion.

Ending

We place all our hope in you, God who is love. Amen.

CHAPTER 5

Make Room for Hope

Call to presence

- God, our hope, you are present with us as we pray.

- As we gather may we attend to your presence, Source of all hope.

- Let us place ourselves in the presence of God, who is the source of our hope.

Prayers

Hebrews 10:23 _____

God, you give us reasons to hope—that is, to see beyond the present with faith in your promise that all will finally be well. Over and over you have proven that you are the source of hope. So, as Paul told the Hebrews, "Let us hold fast to the confession of our hope without wavering, for [Christ] who has promised is faithful."

Many disappointments and disasters would rob us of hope, but you promise to be with us in all our difficulties. We cling to this promise as the reason for our hope. Strengthen us in all that we do now, always-faithful God.

1 Peter 3:13–14 _____

Your word, our God, says: "Now who will harm you if you are eager to do what is good? But even if you do suffer for doing what is right, you are blessed. Do not fear what they fear, and do not be intimidated." If we hold fast to your word, your truth, and your light, hope will shine in our heart. This is your promise.

We need this hope as we gather together. Help us to be eager to do what is right and good. Bless us even when we run into difficulties. When we are fearful, may we remember your power and grace. Stay with us, God of all hope.

Psalm 119:116 _____

My God,

> As you have promised—
> sustain me that I may live;
> Disappoint me not in my hope.

We can only live fully if we act according to your light, so shine your light into our darkness. We will always be disappointed if you, God, are not at the center of our efforts, so keep us focused on your presence. In your light and presence, we can go forward in hope. Sustain us that we may live.

Jeremiah 29:11–14 _____

God of all truth, open my ears to hear what you spoke through Jeremiah: "For surely I know the plans I have for you, says [God], plans for your welfare and not for harm, to give you a future with hope. . . . When you search for me, you will find me; if you seek me with all your heart, I will let you find me."

These words are consoling, our God, for your plans for us are not always immediately clear. Even so, we want to hope in your words. Fill us with hope. Help us to find you, Source of all goodness.

Lamentations 3:22–24 _____

Even when your people were in exile in Babylon, they knew that they could hope in you. So they prayed:

> The steadfast love of the LORD never ceases,
>   [God's] mercies never come to an end;
> they are new every morning;
>   great is your faithfulness.
> "The LORD is my portion," says my soul,
>   "therefore I will hope in [God]."

O God, your steadfast love and mercy still exist for us, though we live many centuries after these lamentations were written. So when we feel separated from you, when we embark on new ventures, when we gather together, help us to remember your mercy and steadfast love. Thus we, too, will hope in you.

Hebrews 6:19 _____

Holy God, you sent hope to us in Jesus. As Paul proclaimed, "We have this hope, a sure and steadfast anchor of the soul, a hope that enters the inner shrine."

Make us steady in our hope by increasing our faith in Jesus. May he be our anchor when all seems lost, when distress and trials seem to overwhelm us, when we face hard decisions and tough issues, and when we are blown about by doubt and fear. Anchor us in Jesus, our hope. This we ask of you as we gather.

Exodus 3:12; 4:12 _____

Almighty God, you were the source of hope for our ancestors, the people of Israel, and you are our source of hope. When Moses argued that he could not possibly confront Pharaoh, you told him, "I will be with you." When he feared that they would not listen to him, you said, "I will be your mouth and teach you what you are to speak."

God, be with us now. Be our mouth and teach us what to speak. Just as you strengthened Moses, strengthen us with the hope that you will always stand with us and guide us. Come, God of all hope.

Psalm 42:5 _____

Psalm 42 asks:

> Why are you so sad, my soul?
> Why sigh within me?
> Hope in God;
> for I will yet praise my savior and my God.

When we are sad, worried, distrustful, or confused, help us to remember these words, God of light and hope. Instead of groaning or whining, help us to offer praise to you, our God, for all the good in the world, all the bright spots that we might ignore when difficulties seem to be too much to bear. You are our hope and strength. Let us put aside our sadness and sighs. All praise to you, our God.

Psalm 22:1,4 _____

Psalm 22 laments, "My God, my God, why have you deserted me?" but several lines later declares, "In you our ancestors put their trust; / they trusted and you rescued them."

You know that we are funny, fickle people, God. We bemoan our outcast fate. We gripe about our lack of this or that. We are always misunderstood. Then, on further reflection, we have to admit that you have always pulled us away from the fire and delivered us, mostly from ourselves. Come, God, again. May we trust you once again. Once again you will deliver us, because you are ever a God of hope.

Proverbs 24:13–14 _____

Gracious God, one of your proverbs says:

> My child, eat honey, for it is good,
>> and the drippings of the honeycomb are sweet to
>>> your taste.
> Know that wisdom is such to your soul;
>> If you find it, you will find a future,
>> and your hope will not be cut off.

Send us such sweet wisdom so that we may find a future and have rich hope. We know that all wisdom comes from you, our God, and we certainly need it. Guide us in all things, God of hopeful wisdom.

Romans 5:1–2 _____

Merciful God, Jesus came to offer us hope. His Resurrection from the dead conquered death once and for all. So Paul declared, "Therefore, since we are justified by faith, we have peace with God through our Lord Jesus Christ, through whom we have obtained access to this grace in which we stand; and we boast in our hope of sharing the glory of God."

We do stand in grace. Let us never forget that. Especially now as we come together, ground our hope in one fact: that all of us stand in your grace, all of us have a share in your glory.

Romans 5:3–5 _____

Paul tried to encourage the Romans with these words: "Suffering produces endurance, and endurance produces character, and character produces hope, and hope does not disappoint us, because God's love has been poured into our hearts through the Holy Spirit that has been given to us."

We have probably had our share of suffering, some of us more than others. You, God, must judge whether endurance has produced character and hope in us. Whatever the case, you will never disappoint us. Pour your love into our soul to increase our hope. Spirit of God, help us to realize now and always that you are with us to guide us in the ways of hopeful living.

Sirach 2:3–6 _____

We need the hope that only you can give us, God of all goodness. In tough times and also in good times, help us to remember your words in Sirach:

> Cling to [God], . . .
>> so that your last days may be prosperous.
> Accept whatever befalls you,
>> in times of humiliation be patient;
> For gold is tested in the fire
>> and those found acceptable, in the furnace of
>>> humiliation.
> Trust in [God], and [God] will help you;
>> make your ways straight, and hope in [God].

We could all do without the testing of misfortune, but we can have hope in you, our God. Help us now. Guide us as we make our way straight to you.

Matthew 5:3–12 _____

God of all blessings, the greatest blessing that you have sent to us is Jesus. He assured us that we have reason to hope in the coming of your Reign. As we gather now, may we remember these words of hope and blessing; may they be a challenge and a comfort:

> Blessed are the poor in spirit, for theirs is the kingdom of heaven.
> Blessed are those who mourn, for they will be comforted.
> Blessed are the meek, for they will inherit the earth.
> Blessed are those who hunger and thirst for righteousness, for they will be filled.
> Blessed are the merciful, for they will receive mercy.
> Blessed are the pure in heart, for they will see God.
> Blessed are the peacemakers, for they will be called children of God.
> Blessed are they who are persecuted for righteousness' sake, for theirs is the kingdom of heaven. . . .
> Rejoice and be glad, for your reward is great in heaven.

Romans 8:24–25 _____

God, your servant Paul said: "Now hope that is seen is not hope. For who hopes for what is seen? But if we hope for what we do not see, we wait for it with patience."

This is certainly true, dear God, but it is a hard truth. Not seeing stretches our ability to believe, to hope, and to love. Help us to patiently wait with hope. Your desire for us can only be good. In trials give us patience. In joy give us gratitude. But always keep the fragile seeds of hope growing in our soul until all things are made new in you, our Creator.

Ending

We offer this prayer, confident in the hope that Jesus brings. Amen.

CHAPTER 6

Offer Thanks and Praise

Call to presence

- Let us remember that we are in the holy presence of God.
- Let us recall that our bountiful God is with us today in this place.
- Gracious God, here present, listen as we pray.

Prayers

Psalm 44:8

Living God, we praise you with all our heart. "In you, God, have we gloried all day long, / and we will praise your name forever."

All that is good comes from you, gracious God, as a gift to us. To praise you is the only fitting response. May we never forget that we live and move and have our being because of your creative, loving grace. Praised be your name forever.

1 Corinthians 15:54–57 _____

All praise and thanks to you, Holy One, for sending Christ Jesus to redeem us from sin and death. We declare with Paul:

> "Death has been swallowed up in victory."
> "Where, O death, is your victory?
> Where, O death, is your sting?"
> . . . Thanks be to God, who gives us the victory through our Lord Jesus Christ.

Merciful God, even though we have worries and troubles, you promise ultimate victory for those who trust in you. For this we give you cheerful thanks and grateful praise.

Psalm 89:1–5 _____

We join the psalmist to give you praise, God our hope:

> I will sing the wonders of your love forever, Yahweh;
> I will proclaim your faithfulness to all generations.
> I will declare that your love is steadfast,
> your faithfulness fixed as the heavens.
>
> . . . .
>
> The heavens praise your wonders, Yahweh,
> and the assembly of the holy ones exalts your faithfulness.

You do love us, faithful God. Over and over you have shown your mercy and kindness to us. We offer you praise and thanks from a grateful heart.

Colossians 3:15–16 _____

God, your messenger Paul reminds us: "Be thankful. Let the word of Christ dwell in you richly; teach and admonish one another in all wisdom; and with gratitude in your hearts sing psalms, hymns, and spiritual songs to God."

We do give you our gratitude, God of wonder, God of life. For all your blessings, we thank you. For all that is, we offer praise. With a hopeful heart, we invite your word to inspire us to always give you thanks and blessings.

Psalm 104:1–2,24 _____

All creation praises you, living and true God. As we gather we offer you our praise, too.

> Bless Yahweh, O my soul.
> How great you are, Yahweh, my God!
> You are clothed in majesty and splendor,
> wrapped in a robe of light!
>
> . . . .
>
> Yahweh, how many are the works you have created,
> arranging everything in wisdom!

We lift our heart and mind to you, our Creator. Your divine wisdom and love show forth in all the wonders of your creation. Thanks be to you, God of endless glory.

1 Thessalonians 5:16–19 _____

In your holy presence, God, we gather to give you praise and thanks in all that we do. As the Scriptures tell us: "Rejoice always, pray without ceasing, give thanks in all circumstances; for this is the will of God in Christ Jesus for you. Do not quench the Spirit."

And so, Holy One, we do rejoice in your faithfulness and unending love for us. We pray with these words of thanks and praise. We invite the Holy Spirit to flood our soul with light and hope and love. Praise and thanks to you, God of glory.

Psalm 108:1–4 _____

God of our life, we join our voices to those of the psalmist, proclaiming:

> My heart is ready, O God;
> I will sing, sing your praise
> and make music with all my soul.
> Awake, lyre and harp.
> I will wake the dawn.
> I will praise you, Yahweh, among the peoples;
> among the nations I will give thanks,
> for your love reaches to the heavens
> and your faithfulness to the skies.

As we gather may only words of gratefulness and praise be in our heart and on our lips.

Luke 19:37 _____

Saving God, when Jesus entered Jerusalem triumphantly, the disciples "began to praise God joyfully with a loud voice for all the deeds of power that they had seen."

Every day you show us fresh signs and wonders. If we have the vision to notice them, we experience the miracles of love that show your care for us: acts of simple kindness, the glories of the natural world, the embraces of loved ones. For all these gifts, we offer grateful thanks and praise to you, gracious God.

Psalm 75:1,9 _____

We give you thanks, O God; we give you thanks.
Your name is brought very near to us
in the story of your wonderful deeds.

. . . .

But I will glorify God forever;
I will sing praises to the God of Jacob and Rachel.

This gathering gives you praise and thanks, God of our ancestors. Just as you performed wonderful deeds in times past, so you still create the world, inviting all of us to faith, hope, and love. For your saving grace and marvelous works, thanks be to you, God of endless glory.

James 5:13 _____

Forgiving God, through the Resurrection of Christ you have set us free from the slavery of sin and death. And so we give you thanks and praise. As Paul says: "Are any cheerful? They should sing songs of praise."

With your support and blessings, how can we not be cheerful? You are always at our side, even as we rise to resurrected glory with Christ Jesus. All praise, thanks, and glory to you, God of all goodness and gifts.

Psalm 100:1–5 _____

Holy One, as we come together now, we begin with words of thanks and praise from Psalm 100:

> Shout for joy to God,
> all the lands!
> Serve God with gladness!
> Come into God's presence with joyful singing!
>
> . . . .
>
> . . . We belong to God;
> we are God's people and the sheep of God's pasture.
> Enter God's gates with thanksgiving
> and the courts with praise!
> Give thanks to God; bless God's name!
> For Yahweh is good;
> God's steadfast love endures forever,
> and God's faithfulness to all generations.

Luke 2:20 _____

Saving God, you led the shepherds to the humble birthplace of Jesus. In faith they recognized their savior. As the Scriptures say, they "returned, glorifying and praising God for all they had heard and seen."

How much more should we give you glory and praise. Jesus Christ has risen in glory. Your Holy Spirit dwells with us to guide and inspire us. And so we gather in your name, blessing and thanking you with a joyful heart, God who loves us.

Psalm 136:1–4,24–25 _____

We gather to praise and thank you, God, our creator. In the words of Psalm 136:

> We give thanks to you, Yahweh, for you are good.
> Your love is everlasting!
> We give thanks to you, God of gods.
> Your love is everlasting!
> You alone do great wonders.
> Your love is everlasting!

Your wisdom made the heavens.
Your love is everlasting!

. . . .

You provide for all living creatures.
Your love is everlasting!
Give thanks to the God of Heaven,
for God's love is everlasting!

Philippians 1:3–11 _____

As we gather in your presence, our God, we thank you for the
support and example of your holy people. We pray with Paul,
"I thank my God every time I remember you, . . . because of
your sharing in the gospel. . . . This is my prayer, that your
love may overflow more and more . . . so that in the day of
Christ you may be pure and blameless, having produced the
harvest of righteousness that comes through Jesus Christ for
the glory and praise of God."

God, you called us into community. We do not follow
Christ alone. May we praise and thank you by our overflowing
love for one another and by our good life. This is our prayer to
you, our God.

Psalm 148:1–3,11–13 _____

Praise God from the heavens;
praise God in the heights;
praise God, all you angels;
praise God, all you heavenly hosts.
Praise God, sun and moon;
praise God, all you shining stars.

. . . .

Let the rulers of the earth and all peoples
and all the judges of the earth—
young men too, and maidens,
old women and men—
praise the name of God
whose name alone is exalted;
and who has raised the fortunes of the people.

Praise is our prayer to you, God of the universe, as we come together in the name of Jesus.

Ending

All praise and thanks to you, our God. Amen. Alleluia.

CHAPTER 7

Seek Wisdom

Call to presence

- Come, Holy Wisdom, be present with us now as we pray.

- The God who knows and understands all things is with us.

- Come, Holy Spirit, and send your light upon us.

Prayers

Psalm 1:1–2 _____

May we remember the advice of Psalm 1, "Oh, the joy of those / . . . [who] delight in the law of Yahweh." As we go about our time together, may these words stay with us. After all, God's law tells us to love one another, to act with kindness and justice. Love, kindness, and justice truly lead to happiness.

God, grant us the grace to delight in your wisdom. Lead us to happiness. Help us to be mindful that if we expect happiness in our world, we must start with delighting in and acting according to your law of love.

Job 11:6 _____

God, source of all wisdom, the Scriptures tell us that "wisdom is many-sided."

All too often we seek simple answers to complex questions. Wisdom teaches us that most issues have many sides. Help us to be dissatisfied with oversimplification, with pat answers, with snap judgments. Lead us instead to stay with our discernment so that we can see issues in all their facets. Give us steadfastness until your light breaks through our confusion.

Proverbs 1:20–23 _____

May we heed your words, gracious God, when you declare:

> Wisdom cries out in the street;
> in the squares she raises her voice.
>
> . . . .
> "How long, O simple ones, will you love being simple?
>
> . . . .
> Give heed to my reproof;
> I will pour out my thoughts to you."

God, your wisdom cries out from all our experiences, but mostly we ignore it. Grant us the grace to pray with our experience, to learn from it, to see your holy hand working within all life. You do pour out your thoughts to us through the advice of friends, the cycles of nature, the Scriptures, and the voice of our heart. May we listen well.

Proverbs 11:2–3 _____

The Scriptures say: "Wisdom is with the humble. / The integrity of the upright guides them."

God of all truth, grant us the wisdom of humility—that is, help us to learn from anyone and to listen to truth wherever it may be found. The humble recognize that everyone has some of your divine light shining out to the rest of us. None of us has all the answers to life's questions. Give us a humble heart so that we may attain wisdom that will guide us with integrity.

Proverbs 19:8 _____

Holy One, we need wisdom and understanding. This is what you will for us. As the Scriptures make clear, "To get wisdom is to love oneself; / to keep understanding is to prosper."

Pour forth your spirit into us, Holy One, so that we keep our eyes, ears, and heart open to your wisdom, wherever it may be found. Urge us to "keep understanding," to keep learning, to attend to your presence in our experiences and in our neighbors. In this way, Creator of us all, we will not only gain wisdom but love ourselves as well.

Ecclesiastes 9:16–18 _____

As we gather in your presence, merciful God, we pray for wisdom, recalling the words from the Scriptures:

> Wisdom is better than might. . . .
> > The quiet words of the wise are more to be heeded
> > > than the shouting of a ruler among fools.
> Wisdom is better than weapons of war.

Indeed, without wisdom we resort to power and weapons of war. In all our dealings together, may we recall these words from the Scriptures and seek wisdom together rather than power over one another or overprotection of our point of view. Help us to be seekers of your wisdom.

Matthew 11:19 _____

Holy Wisdom, you share your wisdom with all of us if we have an open mind and a willing heart. May we constantly remember the words of the Scriptures that say, "yet wisdom is vindicated by her deeds." This passage is consolation and challenge to us.

If we act according to your holy will, God, our deeds will eventually prove to be good. That is the consolation. The challenge is that only in right action do we manifest the wisdom of your will. Divine Wisdom, come to us, show us your will and how to do it.

Acts of the Apostles 6:3 _____

God of all creation, when the early Christians needed to choose deacons to serve the community, the twelve told them to select people "full of the Spirit and of wisdom."

Your Spirit and your wisdom go together. Wisdom comes through your Holy Spirit, giving us light and energy. So come, Holy Spirit, come. Bring your wisdom so that we may be light to the world and a servant to our community. Come, Holy Spirit, come.

1 Corinthians 1:20–21

God, your wisdom defies conventional wisdom. Your prophet Paul told the people: "Where is the one who is wise? . . . Has not God made foolish the wisdom of the world? For since, in the wisdom of God, the world did not know God through wisdom, God decided, through the foolishness of our proclamation, to save those who believe."

Christ is wisdom, even though his love for poor people seemed foolish, his challenge to the status quo seemed foolish, and the cross seemed foolish. Your ways, our God, are not human ways. May we have the true wisdom to follow the example of Jesus even though his way of life may seem to have been naive foolishness.

Luke 21:15

Our Savior, Jesus Christ, promised the disciples that when they were attacked, "I will give you words and a wisdom that none of your opponents will be able to withstand or contradict."

Holy One, send us this same wisdom. Give us words of power, power for good. In disagreements and in times of harmony, may our words be your wisdom, wisdom that we can trust. Spirit of God, fill us with your holy wisdom.

Ephesians 3:10–11

Your wisdom, all-powerful God, is wider and deeper than we can ever fully comprehend. Even so, you grace us with the ability to spread your word. This is why we gather as a community. As Paul says: "Through the church the wisdom of God in its rich variety might now be made known. . . . This was in accordance with the eternal purpose [of God]."

Paul tells us that we are called to make known God's wisdom, but this wisdom has rich variety. Gracious God, help us to speak your word—but humbly—realizing that your word may be spoken in a variety of ways. Humbly, because we only have a part of your word to proclaim. May we always play an active part in your eternal purpose.

Colossians 2:2–3 _____

Creator of the universe, you sent wisdom to us in the person of Christ. Jesus is the key to all wisdom and understanding, as Paul says, "all the riches of assured understanding and . . . the knowledge of God's mystery . . . is Christ himself, in whom are hidden all the treasures of wisdom and knowledge."

And so your people gather in the presence of Christ to seek this wisdom and knowledge. May we attend to your word and example, then go and do likewise. Thus we, too, may have all the riches of understanding that you promised in the Incarnation. Blessings and praise to you, Source of wisdom.

Proverbs 3:19–22 _____

God, your wisdom is creative. As the Scriptures say:

The LORD by wisdom founded the earth;
    by understanding [God] established the heavens;

. . . .

My child . . .
    keep sound wisdom and prudence,
and they will be life for your soul.

All wisdom comes from you, our God. It is not passive but moves to acts of creativity. Grant us your wisdom, our Creator, so that we may build your Reign here on earth, a Reign of peace, justice, and charity. Truly this creative wisdom will be life for our soul and for the world.

2 Timothy 2:1,7 _____

All understanding comes from you, kind God. With that understanding comes the call to share it. Paul told his friend

Timothy: "Be strong in the grace that is in Christ Jesus. . . . Think over what I say, for the Lord will give you understanding in all things."

God, grace us with understanding of all that is important: how to love, how to serve, how to listen to your will, how to live in harmony with one another. May we think over what you have told us in the Scriptures and what you tell us through one another. Make us wise and strong in Christ Jesus.

1 Corinthians 8:1 _____

Saving God, bless us with true wisdom, not just knowledge. As the Scriptures say, "Knowledge puffs up, but love builds up."

Love walks hand in hand with wisdom. The stronger our embrace of Christ, that much more will we grow in wisdom. So, God, draw us ever closer to you in love. Then we will come to the true light of your wisdom. Following your light we may truly build up the Body of Christ.

Ending

This prayer we offer to you, Spirit of wisdom and understanding. Amen.

CHAPTER 8

Servant Leadership

Call to presence

- Shepherd of souls, be with us now as we gather in your name.

- God of gods, but servant of us all, be present with us now.

- Let us attend to the presence of God, our savior.

Prayers

Isaiah 42:1–4 _____

Saving God, you sent the prophet Isaiah to guide your people. Through him you told us what it means to be a servant leader:

> I have put my spirit upon [my servant]
> he will bring forth justice to the nations.

> . . . .

> [My servant] will not grow faint or be crushed
> until he has established justice in the earth.

God, you have called all of us to be servant leaders, each in our own way. As we come together, may we keep your words clearly before us: we are to lead your people to justice. Strengthen us as you did Isaiah and all the prophets.

Mark 10:43–45 _____

God of mercy and forgiveness, Jesus showed us how to serve, and reminded his followers what service is all about: "Whoever wishes to become great among you," he said, "must be your servant, and whoever wishes to be first among you must be slave of all. For the Son of Man came not to be served but to serve."

Truly, God, you have given us the example of servant leadership in Jesus, who healed us, drove out evil from our midst, and traveled about preaching the Good News with nowhere to lay his head. He became the servant of all. May we have the grace to follow in his footsteps in all that we do.

Luke 4:18 _____

Jesus described his ministry of service and leadership this way:

The Spirit of the Lord is upon me,

. . . .

to bring good news to the poor.
. . . to proclaim release to the captives
and recovery of sight to the blind,
to let the oppressed go free.

We followers of Jesus have been blessed with his ministry. We cannot do it without your grace, Holy One. Send us your Spirit that we might take up the tasks of Christian service: healing, teaching, liberating. Then we, too, may say that the Spirit of the Lord is with us. Come, Jesus, send forth your Spirit.

John 12:26 _____

Following Jesus demands your grace, God of all goodness. Without it we could not be the people of service spoken of in the Gospel: "Whoever serves me must follow me, and where I am, there will my servant be also."

We claim to be your servants, Creator of the universe. But do we serve your people like Jesus did? Sometimes, yes; sometimes, no. Send your Spirit into us so that we may follow you, leading one another to service.

Isaiah 65:13–14 _____

Holy One, you call us not only to be servants but to be cheerful servants. The Scriptures say, "My servants shall rejoice, / . . . my servants shall sing for gladness of heart."

When we do your holy will, joy and gladness fill us. So, merciful God, make your will clear to us, and then strengthen us to do it. We gather in your name, and so we pledge ourselves to service of your Reign. May we serve your people with a cheerful heart.

Romans 12:10–13 _____

Servant leadership is not such a mystery, holy and living God. As Paul told the Romans: "Love one another with mutual affection; outdo one another in showing honor. Do not lag in zeal, be ardent in spirit, serve the Lord. . . . Contribute to the needs of the saints; extend hospitality to strangers."

Loving God, grant us the grace to live Paul's words. May we love, respect, and zealously serve one another, and may we always be hospitable. Let us never forget the great virtue of hospitality to strangers.

1 Peter 4:10 _____

God, you draw us steadily into your embrace. Jesus always welcomed people and let other people welcome him with their hospitality. Paul told the people, "Like good stewards of the manifold grace of God, serve one another with whatever gift each of you has received."

All-wise God, may we likewise serve one another. First, may we appreciate the gifts that you have given us: our talents and skills. You give them to us not only for our own use, but as a means of service. Help us to be good stewards to all our sisters and brothers. Thus we will manifest your manifold grace.

2 Timothy 2:24–25

Divine Teacher, you invite us to serve you by serving your people. The Scriptures instruct us in the ways of servant leadership, "The Lord's servant must not be quarrelsome but kindly to everyone, an apt teacher, patient, correcting opponents with gentleness."

Grace us, our God, with these virtues, so that we may be fitting servants in your name. Temptations to quarrel sometimes beset us even when we gather in your name. With your grace and in your name, may we listen and try to understand one another and be kind.

Colossians 1:1,23

Creator of the universe, your servant Paul always greeted the people as your servant. Even though he was a great leader and teacher, he knew his power came from you. He said, "Paul, an apostle of Christ Jesus by the will of God, . . . became a servant of this gospel."

By our baptism we have been made servants of the Gospel, too. Rather than being stripped of power, we have been given power to preach, teach, and care for one another. Like Paul we have the grace to be servant leaders. May we always embrace our power as servants of this Gospel.

Luke 1:38

God of wonder, you gave us an example of serving and leading when you invited Mary to be the mother of Jesus. By accepting to do your will and be fruitful, she became empowered to help bring about the salvation of all people. Yet she knew herself to be a servant, "Here am I, the servant of the Lord," she said. "Let it be with me according to your word."

Being a servant of your word, our God, does not strip us of our dynamism, our energy, our power. On the contrary, our zeal, focus, and strength are only increased. Today we welcome your will for us. Help us to understand it clearly and to do it eagerly.

Psalm 68:5–6 _____

> Father of the fatherless, mother of the orphan,
> and protector of the weak is God.
> God gives the forsaken a home in which to dwell
> and leads out the prisoners to freedom.

God, our protector and liberator, in parenting us and sheltering us, you show us how to serve one another. If we desire to follow in your way, give us the grace to imitate you as protectors of the weak and liberators of captives.

Matthew 18:10–12 _____

Divine Shepherd, may we always remember Jesus' words about caring for one another: "Take care that you do not despise one of these little ones. . . . If a shepherd has a hundred sheep, and one of them has gone astray, does he not leave the ninety-nine on the mountains and go in search of the one that went astray?"

We may be tempted to look after people who are easily served. Help us, gracious God, to seek the lost sheep and the little ones: children, poor people, our elders who need assistance, victims of injustice—all your people for whom Jesus came. Guide us to be shepherds in the image of Jesus.

2 Corinthians 2:17 _____

Holy One, you lead us to fullness of life. Through your holy word, we are called to do likewise. As Paul says, "We are not peddlers of God's word like so many; but in Christ we speak as persons of sincerity, as persons sent from God and standing in [God's] presence."

May all our words be spoken in sincerity, kindness, honesty, and hope. You, God, do not want us to manipulate people's feelings and play on their weaknesses in order to peddle your word. Servant leadership demands simple speech. Give us words to speak that come only from you.

Luke 6:39–40

Jesus gave us this truth: "Can a blind person guide a blind person? Will not both fall into a pit? A disciple is not above the teacher, but everyone who is fully qualified will be like the teacher."

Holy One, you sent Jesus to be our teacher and guide. May we imitate him, leading with good judgment, generosity, and care. Energize us to study your holy word and to make it part of ourselves so that we will be more like our teacher, Christ Jesus. Then we can lead and teach as Jesus did.

Mark 16:15–18

Before he ascended, Jesus told us: "Go into all the world and proclaim the good news to the whole creation. . . . By using my name they will cast out demons; they will speak in new tongues; . . . they will lay their hands on the sick, and they will recover."

In Jesus' name we have great power for good. Source of all power, strengthen our faith so that we do in deed proclaim the good news, expel evil, communicate effectively, and heal. Through baptism we have been called your disciples. May we now and always act like disciples.

Ending

This prayer we offer in the name of Jesus, servant of all, divine leader of all. Amen.

CHAPTER 9

Set Our Eyes on Faith

Call to presence

- With trust in your love, we pray to you, our God.

- As a believing people, we gather in prayer.

- In faith let us remember the presence of God.

Prayers

Hebrews 11:1 _____

Holy God, we gather in your name. May our coming together be a time of faith. As Saint Paul reminded the Hebrew people, "Faith is the assurance of things hoped for, the conviction of things not seen."

Send your grace of faith so that even though we do not know the outcome of our time together, we may have hope that all will be well. Give us conviction so that if we allow your grace to work in us, we can do good together and make this world a more just, peaceful, and charitable place.

Ephesians 2:8 _____

Loving God, may we always remember that all life, all goodness, all truth come from you. Even our faith is a pure gift.

Paul reminds us, "By grace you have been saved through faith, and this is not your own doing; it is the gift of God."

Thank you, God, for the gift of faith. Help us to gain courage from the faith that you give us. May we turn to you with a steady gaze and an open heart, having clearly before us the fact that faith is not something we can borrow from others, achieve for ourselves, or earn by our hard work. It is a gift that we receive with a grateful heart.

Psalm 145:13–14 _____

God, our creator, may your faithfulness strengthen our faith in you. As the psalmist says:

> Yahweh, you are faithful in all your words
> and holy in all your works.
> You lift up all who are falling
> and raise up all who are bowed down.

We regularly fall down, and troubles bow us down. But you are faithful, God, not only in words but also in works. You brought the Israelites out of slavery and sent Jesus to save us from the bondage of death and sin. Give us eyes to see your faithful deeds in salvation history and in all that is good and true and beautiful in our world. May we set our heart on you, faithful God.

Hebrews 12:1–2 _____

God of tender mercy, throughout history you have made covenants with your people. The most powerful sign of your faithfulness to these covenants was Jesus Christ, whom you sent to save us. Jesus' life, sacrifice, and Resurrection were a seamless expression of your eternal love for us. "Let us," as Paul says, "[look] to Jesus the pioneer and perfecter of our faith."

Perfect our faith in Christ so that Christ can lead us to a life of love and hope, peace and justice, moderation and courage. All praise and thanks to you, Source of our faith, Creator, Redeemer, and Sanctifier.

Luke 7:22 _____

Divine Life-Giver, our faith in you is not misplaced. Your love for us is revealed in the deeds of Jesus and of all those who follow in his footsteps. We can have confident faith in you because Jesus and those of rich faith show us your love when, "the blind receive their sight, the lame walk, the lepers are cleansed, the deaf hear, the dead are raised, the poor have good news brought to them."

Deepen and strengthen our faith so that we, too, may be healers and bringers of the Good News that you have given us in Jesus Christ.

Matthew 2:10–11 _____

God of wonder, God of light, you opened the hearts of the Magi to receive Jesus as the hope for the world. As the Gospel says: "When they saw that the star had stopped, they were overwhelmed with joy. On entering the house, they saw the child with Mary, his mother; and they knelt down and paid him homage."

Jesus, the star of faith, is always shining for us if we only have faith to see him. Give us a heart open to see and believe like the Magi. Fill us with the joy of faith. May your light change us and bring to birth in us a passionate love for Christ. As we gather may our time be an act of homage to our God and Savior.

Romans 10:14–17 _____

Holy One, may we be bearers of the Good News to one another. Strengthen and deepen our faith so that we can support and enlighten the faith of our brothers and sisters. Help us always to remember Paul's words to the Romans: "How are they to believe in one of whom they have never heard? And how are they to hear without someone to proclaim him? . . . As it is written, 'How beautiful are the feet of those who bring good news!' . . . So faith comes from what is heard, and what is heard comes through the word of Christ."

May we bring this word of Christ to one another and to all who hear us.

Psalm 119:105–108 _____

O God,

> Your word is a lamp for my steps,
> a light to my path.
> I resolve and have taken an oath
> to follow your just decrees.
> I am sorely afflicted.
> Give me life according to your word.
> Accept the willing praise of my mouth, O God,
> and teach me your decrees.

Surely, God, your word is a light that guides us. It is life-giving. May we study your word, pray and meditate upon it, and learn its wisdom and truth. In this way we can live in the fullness of your grace. We praise and thank you for your holy word, which is the lamp of our faith.

John Newton _____

May the words of this hymn—this song of faith—come from our soul to you, God of infinite mercy:

> Amazing grace, how sweet the sound
> that saved a wretch like me.
> I once was lost, but now I'm found;
> was blind, but now I see.
>
> 'Twas grace that taught my heart to fear,
> and grace my fear relieved.
> How precious did that grace appear
> the hour I first believed.

Give us such passionate faith. We have been lost and blind. Only your holy grace can guide us right and give us the sight of faith. Grant us, too, your amazing grace.

Philemon 1:4–6 _____

God of compassion, fill us with faith so that we may share our faith with one another and with all people. Paul told his friend Philemon: "I always thank my God because I hear of your love for all the saints and your faith toward the Lord Jesus. I pray that the sharing of your faith may become effective when you perceive all the good that we may do for Christ."

As we gather may we take joy in the faith of one another. Grant us, God, the grace to share our faith in Christ. And so strengthened, may our faith lead us to good both in word and in deed.

1 Peter 1:8–9 _____

Gracious God, we pray for a more certain and steady faith in you and in Christ Jesus. Peter reminds us, "Even though you do not see [Christ] now, you believe in him and rejoice with an indescribable and glorious joy, for you are receiving the outcome of your faith, the salvation of your souls."

We do believe in Christ, but in the midst of our fears, worries, doubts, and distractions, our faith is tested. The joy escapes us. Send forth your grace, God, so that we may believe and thus experience the joy of firm faith.

Galatians 3:25–26 _____

Living God, you give us unconditional love and offer us the freedom to give love in return. This is possible through the coming of Jesus. As the Epistle to the Galatians says, "Now that faith has come, we are no longer subject to a disciplinarian, for in Christ Jesus you are all children of God through faith."

We are your children, God, our creator. May our faith be as that of children who believe in loving parents. May our faith be simple, open, honest, and trusting. And may we love you.

Acts of the Apostles 15:9 _____

All-wise and loving God, our faith should draw us together, not tear us apart, although it does not always work that way. When the early Christians objected to Gentiles joining them, Peter the Apostle told them that "cleansing their hearts by faith [God] has made no distinction between them and us."

We are called to be one people in faith. Draw us together, God, so that we care for one another, listen to one another, and respect one another as your children—no matter the color of our skin, the years we have lived, the accent in our speech, or the money in our pockets. May our faith make us one.

Luke 8:48

Let us remember Jesus' healing words. Whenever he cured someone, he told them, "Your faith has made you well; go in peace." Over and over Jesus said the same thing: faith does heal us.

God, you want us to be whole and healthy. Strengthen us in faith so that our faith will heal us in whatever ways we need to be healed. May our shared faith heal any divisions among us, any scars from old arguments and lingering grudges. Give us the grace of healing faith so that we may be the hale and hearty people of God, the strong and vigorous Body of Christ.

2 Thessalonians 1:3

God, your servant Paul always rejoiced in the growing faith of the communities. He told the Thessalonians, "We must always give thanks to God for you, brothers and sisters, as is right, because your faith is growing abundantly, and the love of everyone of you for one another is increasing."

Faith and love go together because belief in Christ manifests itself in love. What would Paul say of our gathering? Is our faith growing? Is our love obvious? Holy One, help us to grow in abundant faith, too. And may our faith flow out in equally abundant love for one another.

Ending

As a people seeking to grow in faith, we offer this prayer in Jesus' name. Amen.

CHAPTER 10

Take Courage

Call to presence

- All-powerful and loving God, you dwell within us. Hear our prayer.

- In our weakness and strength, you are with us, Holy One.

- Let us recall that the Creator of the universe comes among us now.

Prayers

Adapted from Sirach 2:1–6 _____

All-good God, it is fitting that the word *courage* comes from the French word for "heart." May we be of good and strong heart in all things and recall your words:

> Those who serve God
> must be ready to be tested.
> Set your heart in the right direction and be strong.
> In times of disaster, do not weaken.
> Gold is always tested in fire.
> Trust God, and God will help you.
> Hold firm to the good, and hope in God.

May our heart be set in the right direction. Help us to hold firm and be people of goodness and hope.

Adapted from 1 Chronicles 22:11–13 _____

The First Book of Chronicles tells us: "God go with you so that you can successfully build God's place among humanity. May God give you good judgment and understanding. Have strength and courage."

God, with your help we can be strong and courageous. We can make the earth a place where you reign. We can open our heart to you and become people of peace, justice, and virtue. God, you are with us today and every day. Help us to realize your constant strengthening presence with us.

John 16:33 _____

Jesus said to his followers: "In me you may have peace. In the world you face persecution. But take courage; I have conquered the world!"

Living God, it is sometimes hard to believe that Jesus actually did conquer evil and death. Whenever we want to do the right thing, we are met with doubt, criticism, and negativity. Help us to stay true to our convictions and to do good. May the peace you offer calm our fears and, God of all power, give us courage.

Adapted from Acts of the Apostles 27:22–25 _____

During a raging storm at sea, the Apostle Paul told those with him: "Take courage. An angel sent by God told me that God will bring us safely home. So don't be afraid. Be strong and have faith." And, in fact, Paul and the crew made it safely through the storm.

God, you never promised that life would be smooth sailing. But we know that you will bring us through life's storms if we have faith. So strengthen our faith. With faith we can take heart and have courage in the face of discouragement, doubt, or opposition. Bring us through the storms just as you did your Apostle Paul.

1 Corinthians 16:13–14 _____

When Paul wrote to the Christians in Corinth, he told them: "Keep alert, stand firm in your faith, be courageous, be strong. Let all that you do be done in love."

God of goodness, loving requires courage. Courage comes from our faith that you stand with us and support us. Make our faith stronger and stronger so that all our actions can be motivated by love and not by fear. Give us a courageous heart.

Ephesians 6:10–11 _____

"Be strong in [God] and in the strength of [God's] power," Paul says. "Put on the whole armor of God." Protecting God, we do need your power and strength to have the courage we need in our struggle with evil.

You, God, are courage and power. Indeed, only in you can we survive amid the temptations that surround us on every side: the temptations to greed, deceit, hatred, cheating, and so on. Help us to put on the armor that you give us with your grace: courage, kindness, honesty, patience, and selflessness. Then we can join you to fight the good fight.

2 Chronicles 32:7–8 _____

God, I pray for the courage to enter into controversy and conflict, always considering your ever abiding life and love. When we approach difficulties, let us remember the words that God spoke: "Be strong and of good courage. Do not be afraid or dismayed . . . for with us is the LORD our God, to help us and to fight our battles."

May we never forget your promise always to aid and assist us regardless of the difficulty at hand. In particular, today we need courage in this struggle . . . Guide us; give us courage.

2 Corinthians 5:1,17 _____

Eternal God, may we always be moved to courage as we pray with Paul: "For we know that if the earthly tent we live in is destroyed, we have a building from God, a house not made with hands, eternal in the heavens. . . . If anyone is in Christ, there is a new creation: everything old has passed away; see, everything has become new!"

No matter what the issue, when we call on God for help, it will come to us, because you, God, want us to build your Reign. You are with us in minor scraps and in tragic events, to strengthen and support us. May we be supported by that knowledge as we gather together now.

Peace Prayer of Saint Francis of Assisi _____

May these words of Saint Francis's be our own as we pray for the courage we need to be faithful disciples.

> Loving God, make me an instrument of your peace.
> Where there is hatred, let me sow love;
> Where there is injury, pardon;
> Where there is doubt, faith;
> Where there is despair, hope;
> Where there is darkness, light;
> And where there is sadness, joy.
> O, Divine Teacher, grant that I may not so much seek to
>   be consoled as to console;
> To be understood as to understand;
> To be loved as to love;
> For it is in giving that we receive;
> It is in pardoning that we are pardoned;
> And it is in dying that we are born to eternal life.

Galatians 6:2–9 _____

Gracious God, may I be challenged and given courage by these words: "Bear one another's burdens, and in this way you will fulfill the law of Christ. . . . God is not mocked, for you reap whatever you sow. . . . So let us not grow weary in doing what is right, for we will reap at harvest time, if we do not give up."

We do grow weary of sowing good seeds that seem to be greeted with disagreement, disgust, and disdain. Sometimes we do want to give up. Give us the courage to act together in charity, with perseverance and hope.

Psalm 119:41–43 _____

We pray with the psalmist:

> Let your steadfast love come to me, O God,
> your salvation according to your promise.
> So shall I have an answer for those who reproach me,
> for I trust in your words.
> Leave the word of truth in my mouth—
> for in your decree is my hope.

Steadfast God, leave your words of truth in our mouth, and strengthen our will so that the answer to difficulties is the example of our courage combined with charity. You are our hope; you make perseverance possible.

Matthew 5:13–16 _____

Just God, give us courage to follow the ultimate model of courage, Christ Jesus. May we take to heart his words: "You are the salt of the earth; but if salt has lost its taste, how can its saltiness be restored? . . . You are the light of the world. . . . Let your light shine."

Keep us salty and filled with shining light. May our salt give zest to all we do in your name. May our light be a beacon of hope in despair.

Joshua 1:5–9 _____

God of all power, when Moses died you did not desert our ancestors in faith. Your words to a fearful Joshua apply to us as well: "As I was with Moses, so I will be with you; I will not fail you or forsake you. . . . Only be strong and very courageous, being careful to act in accordance with all the law that my servant Moses commanded you. . . . Be strong and courageous; do not be frightened or dismayed, for the Lord your God is with you wherever you go."

Be with us wherever we go, God of power. As we try to work together for good, guide and strengthen us just as you did Joshua. With your strong presence, may we, too, lead the people of God to the promise of your Reign.

Adapted from 2 Chronicles 15:1–7 _____

Spirit of God, may we hear your words spoken by Azariah: "God is with you, when you abide with God. Seeking, you will find God. . . . While living godlessly, the times were danger-ous, chaotic, and confused. Peoples fought with one another. So, you, have courage. Strengthen your heart and hand, be-cause God will reward your efforts."

Truly we cannot sustain the courage we need to live the good life without God's word to guide us and without God's power to support us. These times can be dangerous, chaotic, and confusing. So we call on you, God, once again for light and strength.

Acts of the Apostles 5:29–32 _____

Life according to your word, O God, certainly is not a walk down easy street. When Peter and the other Apostles were dragged before judges, Peter said: "We must obey God rather than any human authority. The God of our ancestors raised up Jesus, whom you had killed. . . . God exalted him . . . that he might give repentance to Israel and forgiveness of sins. And we are witnesses to these things, and so is the Holy Spirit whom God has given to those who obey [God]." Of course the accusers wanted to kill Peter for blasphemy.

Give us the courage of the Apostles to proclaim your word through speech and actions. If we get into trouble for it, be with us as you were with Peter and the other Apostles. And may we always keep in mind that we must first obey you, God.

Ending

Hear our prayer, God, our strength. Amen.

Acknowledgments *(continued)*

The scriptural material marked "adapted" is freely adapted and is not to be understood or used as an official translation of the Bible.

The psalms in this book are from *Psalms Anew: In Inclusive Language,* compiled by Nancy Schreck and Maureen Leach (Winona, MN: Saint Mary's Press, 1986). Copyright © 1986 by Saint Mary's Press. All rights reserved.

All other scriptural quotations in this book are from the New Revised Standard Version of the Bible. Copyright © 1989 by the Division of Christian Education of the National Council of the Churches of Christ in the United States of America. All rights reserved.